A Table of Offerings

17 Years of Acquisitions
of Egyptian and Ancient
Near Eastern Art by
William Kelly Simpson for the
Museum of Fine Arts, Boston

A Table of Offerings

17 Years of Acquisitions
of Egyptian and Ancient
Near Eastern Art by
William Kelly Simpson for the
Museum of Fine Arts, Boston

Museum of Fine Arts   Boston, Massachusetts

Library of Congress catalogue card
no. 87–50312
Copyright © 1987
by Museum of Fine Arts, Boston,
Massachusetts
Typeset, printed, and bound by
Meriden-Stinehour Press
Designed by Carl Zahn

Cover illustration:
Mummy Shroud. Paint on gessoed linen.
New Kingdom, late Dynasty XVIII–early
Dynasty XIX, about 1310–1275 B.C.
William Stevenson Smith Fund

Foreword

WILLIAM KELLY SIMPSON was appointed curator of Egyptian and Ancient Near Eastern art in the dark days following the sudden death of William Stevenson Smith in 1969. For the next seventeen years, he divided his time between Yale University, where he was professor of Egyptology, and the Museum of Fine Arts, where he carried on the tradition of excellence bequeathed him by his predecessors, Albert M. Lythgoe, George A. Reisner, Dows Dunham, and William Stevenson Smith. During his tenure the department became an important center for Egyptological studies and achieved international recognition for its program of research and publication. This was largely due to Kelly Simpson who, between 1970 and 1986, wrote seventy-eight articles and reviews for scholarly journals, published seven books, coauthored two more, and edited three others, including a second edition of William Stevenson Smith's *Art and Architecture of Ancient Egypt* in the influential Pelican History of Art series. In 1974, Kelly was coauthor with Dows Dunham of the first volume of *Giza Mastabas*, a series recording the Harvard University-Museum of Fine Arts excavations on the Giza plateau between 1904 and 1940, which had brought to the museum magnificent works of art of the Old Kingdom. During the next six years three more volumes in the series appeared under his sole authorship, and *The Offering Chapel of Sekhem-ankh-Ptah in the Museum of Fine Arts, Boston*, documented one of the two Saqqara tomb chapels purchased by the Museum from the Egyptian Antiquities Department in 1904.

In order to devote more of his time to the publications of the department while continuing as professor of Egyptology at Yale, Kelly resigned from his position of curator in 1986. In recognition of his accomplishment and in anticipation of a continuing and fruitful association, the Trustees of the Museum of Fine Arts appointed him consultative curator.

It is Kelly's profound conviction that regardless of the past fortune and success of any museum department, ongoing acquisition is essential to retain the interest of the public, to assure the participation of the staff, and to extend the scope, appeal, and recognition of the collection. Under Kelly's leadership, the department acquired several outstanding Egyptian works of art, among them the statue group of Ukhhotep (p. 17) and the magnificent pectoral of a vulture with outspread wings (p. 21), while simultaneously broadening its holdings in Ancient Near Eastern art. All told some 500 works of art were accessioned by the department between 1970 and 1986; 50 outstanding examples have been selected for inclusion here.

Encouraging and enabling to his younger colleagues in the department, Kelly remains open to new ideas and has always offered his support to students at home and abroad, making the Egyptian collection accessible to all interested researchers. He clearly subscribes to the teaching of the ancient Egyptian sage Ptah-hotep: "Do not be arrogant because of your knowledge, but confer with the ignorant man as with the learned, for the limit of skill cannot be attained, and there is no craftsman who has [fully] acquired his mastery."

Among his many other distinctions, Kelly is president of the International Association of Egyptologists, chairman of the American School of Classical Studies in Athens, and vice president of the American University in Cairo. These distinguished posts entail a considerable expenditure of time and energy, but Kelly has reserves of both to dedicate to his other interests. A fan of the opera, he has drawn on his Egyptological knowledge and written two articles on Verdi's *Aida*.[1] He is an avid collector of modern and contemporary art, and eagerly shares the joy of a new acquisition, whether it be a Vuillard or Bonnard, a Max Beckmann, a Florine Stettheimer, or a Jasper Johns.

This book is dedicated to Kelly Simpson with affection and appreciation for all he has taught us. The works of art illustrated are described in his own words, except in a few instances where Timothy Kendall (pp. 50, 54, 74), Peter Lacovara (pp. 8, 20, 34, 80, 82) or I (pp. 52, 78) have contributed essays. The essays on Ancient Near Eastern art are entirely the work of Timothy Kendall. John Herrmann of the Department of Classical Art and Christopher Ratté of Harvard University generously translated the Greek text on the stela of Heraklides (p. 82). Yvonne Markowitz of Brandeis University, an intern in the Egyptian Department, shared the editorial tasks with me and compiled the bibliography. Special thanks are due Tara Wyman for her careful typing of the manuscript. The book was designed by Carl Zahn, director of publications, and edited by Cynthia Purvis; their assistance is very much appreciated.

EDWARD BROVARSKI
*Curator of Egyptian and
Ancient Near Eastern Art*

[1] William Kelly Simpson, "At the Source," *Opera News* 40 (1976): 32–34; idem, "Mariette and Verdi's *Aida*," *Bulletin of the Egyptological Seminar* 2 (1980): 111–119.

A Table of Offerings

Forepart of a Recumbent Lion

Porphyritic diorite
Egyptian Special Purchase Fund
1980.73

Early Dynastic Period,
Dynasty I–II,
3100–2686 B.C.
H. 5⅛ in. (13 cm)

This crouching lion may belong to a group of stone lion divinities attributed to Gebelein, near Thebes in Upper Egypt, a cult center of some standing. The present example is unique in the group, however, in having once had eyes of a different material inset in the deep sockets. Unlike many Early Dynastic artists, the sculptor of this piece used a hard porphyritic stone with unusually large grayish white inclusions, represented only in several contemporary stone vases. The lion is tensed to spring, lifting its head up to make eye contact with the viewer and wrinkling its nose back in a snarl. Rather than fully sculpting a gaping mouth, the sculptor has only suggested it by incising teeth across the front of the flattened muzzle. The tail, as it normally does for lion sculptures of this date, lies flat along the spine, curling at the tip just below the mane. The piece gives evidence of an interest in the expression of powerful presence and naturalistic effect, later to develop into the monumental sculpture style of the Egyptian Old Kingdom.

Relief from the Tomb of Queen Nofru

From Deir el-Bahri
Limestone
J.H. and E.A. Payne Fund
1973.147

Middle Kingdom,
Dynasty XI,
reign of Mentuhotep II,
about 2040 B.C.
H. 8⅝ in. (22 cm)

In the development of Egyptian relief the royal workshops of Dynasty XI at Deir el-Bahri are held in particular esteem. The tomb of Queen Nofru, sister-wife of Mentuhotep II, at Deir el-Bahri became a show-place for tourists as early as the reign of Queen Hatshepsut of Dynasty XVIII, and many visitors inscribed their names and thoughts on its walls.

The Boston bas-relief belongs to the chapel of Queen Nofru, for the relief in the corridor was executed in sunk relief. The execution of the relief has a gemlike appearance softened by the rounded edges. Two serving women are shown carrying a large pottery vessel on a sling attached to a pole borne on their shoulders. The missing lower part of the vessel and the mat on which it rests can be reconstructed through a scene in Cairo from the same procession. The detail in the strands of hair and the strands of the rope provides an intentional contrast to the smooth surfaces with rounded edges of the bodies and the jar. Of the faces, only that of the first woman, with narrow slanting eyes and elongated paint stripe, strong nose and thick, sharply defined lips, is well preserved.

4

Seated Statuette of an Official

From Asyut
Alabaster
Gift of William Kelly Simpson in memory
of William Stevenson Smith
1971.20

First Intermediate Period or
Dynasty XI,
about 2100–2000 B.C.
H. 11 in. (28 cm)

In its simplified concentration on basic forms, the seated statuette of a now anonymous official from his tomb at Asyut in Middle Egypt is not unlike some sculpture of our own times. Viewed in relation to comparable examples of the Old Kingdom, this statuette of the First Intermediate Period lacks crispness of execution, strict adherence to symmetry, and articulation of detail. Yet these very features give it a powerful character of its own. Other statues of the same series, perhaps by the same sculptor or workshop, are in the collections of museums in Brussels, Cairo, Hannover, and Moscow.

Two Anthropomorphic Vessels

Pottery
William Stevenson Smith Fund
1983.153,154

Middle Kingdom,
Dynasty XI–XII,
about 2133–1786 B.C.
H. 6⅞ in. (17.5 cm)
H. 7⅞ in. (20 cm)

The tradition of anthropomorphic pottery, which first appeared in the Predynastic period, continues to the very end of Dynastic Egypt and into the Roman period. These two somewhat amusing vessels are nonfunctional, since the openings are at the base and the arms cannot have served conveniently as handles. Like examples excavated at Dendera, they may be conveniently designated as mourning pots. The attitude of the hands raised to the head or face is an Egyptian convention for the expression of grief and occurs in many scenes of funerals.

Tomb Relief

From Deir el-Bersheh
Painted limestone
Seth K. Sweetser Fund
1972.984

Middle Kingdom,
Dynasty XII,
reign of Senusert I,
about 1971–1928 B.C.
H. 14½ in. (37 cm)

This fragment of Dynasty XII sunk relief can be assigned to a specific tomb at Bersheh in Middle Egypt. Tomb no. 3 probably belonged to a great chief of the Hare Nome, the nomarch of Upper Egyptian nome 15, Amenemhat, who served Senusert I. His son was the scribe of royal documents, Sep. Our relief bears a text that associates it with the tomb: "incense, alabaster, and linen which his eldest son, beloved of him, of his body, made for him, the scribe of the royal documents Sep, born of Wadjkaues, the vindicated." The lady shown at her offering table holding a lotus blossom is evidently this same Wadjkaues, mother of Sep. She has a characteristic Bersheh profile and slim-waisted figure, and her necklace, amulets, and texts are carefully carved and painted. Unfortunately, at some time in this or the last century, a previous owner of the relief enhanced the colors by overpainting the relief, and it is difficult to determine in every case where the original color is in part preserved and where it has been invented.

Head from a Statue of a Lady

Said to be from Abydos
Possibly acacia wood,
with traces of paint
Marilyn M. Simpson Fund
1986.162

Middle Kingdom,
Dynasty XII,
about 1950 B.C.
H. 8⅞ in. (22.6 cm)

The features of this head of a lady resemble very closely those of the life-size granite statue of Sennuwy, the wife of the nomarch of Asyut, Hepdjefa, in Boston. Hepdjefa and Sennuwy lived in the second reign of Dynasty XII under King Senusert I (about 1971–1928 B.C.). Their statues were discovered far to the south at Kerma in the Sudan, where they had been appropriated by a local chieftain for his own large tomb.

The head is featured by a wig with braided strands over natural hair. The finely carved face, so close to that of the stone statue, exhibits eyebrows in high relief and a strongly marked philtrum. The outer corner of the eye is notched where the cosmetic paint strip that extends it begins. This is a rare feature parallcled in several other statues of the period. Traces of black and white paint remain in the eyes.

Relief of Si-Hathor-Nehy

Perhaps from Kom el-Hisn
Limestone
Robert Jordan Fund
1973.17

Middle Kingdom,
Dynasty XII,
about 1991–1786 B.C.
H. 19¾ in. (50 cm)

This fine relief of the Middle Kingdom belongs to a set of which three other blocks were acquired by the Cairo Museum in 1924. This type of relief was so much prized and admired that it was copied in Dynasties XXV and XXVI. The provenience may be Kom el-Hisn (ancient Imu) in the Eastern Delta, as suggested by the text. The relief comprises the left side of the lintel, while the right side is in Cairo.

Si-Hathor-Nehy is shown seated at the left, facing right, holding a folded cloth that served as a handkerchief in his right hand and a walking stick in his left. He wears a broad collar and a long transparent outer skirt over a simple short skirt. His wig is of the plain shoulder-length variety. The chair on which he sits has a low back and legs that terminate in lion's feet set on low supports. It is provided with a cushion and placed on a low platform.

The influence of Old Kingdom Memphite traditions, with an element of blandness, is clearly seen here. Although the execution is deft and accomplished, internal detail in the figure and hieroglyphs is sparse.

Statue Group of Ukhhotep

From Meir (Cusae)
Black granite
Gift of Egypt Exploration Fund by exchange
1973.87

Middle Kingdom,
Dynasty XII,
about 1897–1843 B.C.
H. 14¾ in. (37.5 cm)

The group of a nomarch of Meir, two of his wives, and a daughter, is especially interesting in that it provides a comparison with a slightly smaller group of the same four individuals in the Egyptian Museum in Cairo. Both statues seem to have been designed for the west wall of the tomb chapel of the nomarch Ukhhotep at Meir. The daughter in the Boston group stands directly in front of her father with feet planted between his. One almost has the sense that the family has been asked by a photographer to stand still in a prescribed position and smile.

The wrap-around skirt of Ukhhotep with its fringe and tie is carefully rendered. The volumes of the bodies and the faces are sensitively treated. The faces are rounded, the eyes are heavily lidded, the latter being a characteristic of the royal and private sculpture of the latter part of the dynasty. Ukhhotep lived in the reign of Senusert II and may have survived into the reign of Senusert III.

Stela of Ameny

Probably from Abydos
Limestone
Seth K. Sweetser Fund
1970.630

Middle Kingdom,
Dynasty XII,
about 1991–1786 B.C.
H. 25¼ in. (64 cm)

The police officer Ameny, also called Ibi-iau, and his wife sit on the left and face his parents on the right across an array of offerings. His two servants in the register below him face his father's two servants. One of the female servants carries a basket with figs or dates, which, in accordance with Egyptian artistic convention, is shown in section with its contents visible as if in X-ray. The scene has a border of *kheker*-ornaments along the top. This modest stela may have formed the rear wall of a small offering chapel or cenotaph at Abydos. The execution of the sunk relief is competent, if not distinguished.

18

Pectoral

Silver, electrum, and gold,
with inlays of carnelian and glass
Egyptian Special Purchase Fund
1981.159

Second Intermediate Period,
Dynasty XIII–XVII,
about 1786–1558 B.C.
H. 4⁵⁄₁₆ in. (11.2 cm)

This splendid inlay originally formed part of the decoration of a royal anthropoid coffin. The pectoral is slightly curved and retains several of the silver pins that held it in place on the breast of the coffin. It takes the form of the vulture-goddess Nekhbet and the cobra-goddess Wadjet, symbolizing the union of Upper and Lower Egypt. The motif is standard on royal coffins from the Second Intermediate Period.

The pectoral is composed of a plain silver backplate made in three separate sections to which are soldered cloisons of electrum wire masked by gold overlays. The inlays consist of carnelian and light and dark blue glass. The glass appears to have been let into the cloisons in a semi-molten state, a technique characteristic of an early stage in the development of true enameling.

Stylistically, the vulture can be classed with examples from the Middle Kingdom, which also show the complex feather pattern of the underwing and a proportionately small head and beak. This implies a date rather early in the Second Intermediate Period, thus making the pectoral one of the earliest examples of the extensive use of glass in Egyptian jewelry.

Statue of the Chief Priest Khety

Probably from Atfih (Aphroditopolis)
Limestone
Egyptian Special Purchase Fund
1982.501

Second Intermediate Period,
Dynasty XVII,
about 1650–1558 B.C.
H. 11¾ in. (30 cm)

Private sculpture of the Second Intermediate Period is insufficiently recognized and identified. This seated statue is closer in conception to the traditions of the late Middle Kingdom in the gaunt structure of the face, the rather artificial wrinkles on the forehead, and the marked naso-labial furrow. These conventions and the folds of flesh on the torso, indicating maturity and well-being, became stock features at this time. The heavy seat cut in one piece with the base, and the rather stolid set of the sandaled feet are typical of the later Second Intermediate Period. Khety was "chief priest" of Hathor, lady of Tpehu, modern Atfih.

Upper Part of a Seated Statue

Gray granite
William E. Nickerson Fund
1972.396

New Kingdom,
Dynasty XVIII,
about 1500 B.C.
H. 11¼ in. (28.5 cm)

The upper half of a seated statue of an official in a dark gray granite has suffered from the effects of natural aging, and the surface of the body is extensively cracked. The face of the subject is set off by a striated wig, which leaves the ears entirely exposed. The lines of hair radiate from the top of the head to create a bang on the forehead. The lines are curved and create an impression of deliberate shaping beneath the ears as they fall to the shoulders. The beard is short, with a distinct downward angle from its end to the base of the throat. The eyes of the statue have a gentle curve of the lower lid and a sharp curve for the upper lid, which is prolonged into a cosmetic line with squared-off end on each side. The eyebrows are treated in plastic fashion and do not curve inward in the center to follow the line of the upper eyelids. Although the official is evidently represented wearing a garment, there is no specific indication of its edges and its presence is inferred from the way the hands cross. The symmetry of the crossed hands and the balancing of the mass of the wig against the V-shape of the face create a sense of quietude and repose. The traditions of the Middle Kingdom were revived at this time, and the characteristic style of Dynasty XVIII still in process of formation.

Drinking Bowl

Blue faience
William E. Nickerson Fund
1977.619

New Kingdom,
mid-Dynasty XVIII,
about 1490–1402 B.C.
Diam. 6⅛ in. (15.7 cm)

Vessels of Egyptian blue faience are among the most appealing objects of the decorative arts from the Second Intermediate Period onward. The bowls were used at banquets, and servants would have poured wine over the rapidly but deftly sketched fishes nibbling on the stems of lotus buds growing from the central pool. Naturally adapted to the surface of the interior of the bowl, the swirling concentric design contrasts with the familiar processional scenes on tomb and temple walls. The deep cerulean blue glaze with designs made from manganese is characteristic of this ware.

Fragmentary Statue of Ahmose called Patjenna

Probably from Karnak
Black granite
Edward J. and Mary S. Holmes Fund
1972.359

New Kingdom,
Dynasty XVIII,
probably reign of Thutmose III,
about 1450 B.C.
H. 14⅞ in. (38 cm)

About three-quarters life-size, this magnificent portrait of Ahmose called Patjenna, son of the viceroy of Nubia Ahmose Turo, was part of a pair statue of the official and his wife seated on a chair with a low backrest. Parts of each side of the chair or throne are also preserved. The official's face is round and is set off by a double wig that covers the upper part of the ears. The parallel lines of both parts of the wig in the statue, with their sweep behind the shoulder, have the effect of setting off the face within a recessed frame. The left arm is raised, with the hand extending from a sleeve and holding the traditional napkin. This sleeve is the only indication of a garment. The statue imparts a feeling of self-assurance and confidence without any real sense of introspection or inner tension.

Ahmose Patjenna was a scribe of the divine offerings of Amen, the son of the viceroy of Nubia named Ahmose Turo, and the grandson of the viceroy of Nubia named Ahmose Si-Tayit. From the text on its seat it seems that he exercised his office on behalf of the great temple of Amen at Karnak.

Stela of Ahmose

Limestone
Egyptian Special Purchase Fund
1981.2

New Kingdom,
Dynasty XVIII,
about 1438–1402 B.C.
H. 19½ in. (49.5 cm)

Under the pair of eyes the owner of the stela, the chief of metalworkers Ahmose and his wife sit on two elaborate wooden chairs facing a table piled high with offerings of food and flowers. Before them stands their eldest son Meny, his right arm raised in a gesture of invocation as he recites a prayer that "all fresh food offerings and a sweet breeze from the north wind" may come forth for their spirits. A younger son, Tjuroy, sits alongside his parents' chair, smelling a lotus. Below this scene other members of the family enjoy the banquet. A third son sits in front of a small table of offerings next to a group of Ahmose's daughters. One of them turns to her companion to offer a mandrake fruit for a taste or sniff.

Head of a Deity

Probably from Karnak
Gray-black granite with red specks
Gift of Heinz Herzer by exchange
44.28/1979.42

New Kingdom,
Dynasty XVIII
reign of Amenhotep III,
about 1402–1363 B.C.
H. 7⅞ in. (20 cm)

In 1944 the museum acquired by exchange from the Peabody Museum of Harvard University the right side of the head of a statue of the reign of Amenhotep III. The statue had probably been made for use in the great temple complex of Karnak. At some time the head was broken from the torso, and the left side of the face was lost. The larger fragment of the head was acquired at Karnak in 1859 by Mrs. J. H. Wells and purchased by the Peabody Museum in 1879. The illustration of this piece in an exhibition catalogue published in 1977 led to the startling discovery that a fragment very similar in style offered at auction in New York in 1976 was actually part of the missing section of the head in the Boston Museum. This piece was acquired for the museum in 1979 and the fragments reunited, as may be seen from the illustration.

The head is of outstanding workmanship. The almond-shaped eyes characteristic of the reign are extended by a broad cosmetic line squared off at the ends. The eyebrows are rendered sculpturally by a stripe in relief that curves over the eyes and terminates just above the end of the cosmetic line. The full lips are edged, and the philtrum is clearly marked. There is the overall beatific expression in the face shared by statues of deities. For this reason one is tempted to regard the head as coming from a divine statue.

Figure Vase

Ceramic
Frank B. Bemis Fund
1985.336

New Kingdom,
Dynasty XVIII,
about 1490–1363 B.C.
H. 5½ in. (14 cm)

This rare and beautiful object belongs to a group of small sculptural ceramic vessels that were produced in Egypt between the reigns of Thutmose III and Amenhotep III. Known collectively as "figure vases," they represent the highest achievement of the Egyptian potter's art and must have been produced by a few specialized and highly skilled craftsmen. They were assembled from segments cast in multiple-piece molds, with additional elements added by hand. The exterior surface was then carefully burnished to remove seams and provide a glossy finish. Such figure vases in the form of a mother and child may have served as containers for human milk, an ingredient often called for in medical texts and used in remedies for insomnia and infertility.

Upper Part of a Statue

Gray-black granite
Egyptian Curator's Fund
1972.360

New Kingdom
Dynasty XVIII,
reign of Amenhotep III
about 1402–1363
H. 6½ in. (16.5 cm)

Since only the upper part of the statue is preserved, it is not entirely certain whether the owner was represented seated, as seems likely, or standing. The anonymous official wears a clearly marked garment with short sleeves and a characteristic loop tie, actually a drawstring with the ends showing. The garment is shown in statuary and relief of the latter half of the dynasty. The damaged nose was fairly broad. The lips are carefully rendered, the sharply defined philtrum tends to shape the upper lip, the lower lip is full in the center, and both lips have the carved edging that indicates the work of a master sculptor. The clearly marked ends of the lips show traces of the drill. The overall impression is that of a full classic head of the reign of Amenhotep III, but the eyes, eyebrows, nose, and mouth are somewhat large and heavy for the scale of the sculpture.

Amarna Relief

Probably from Tell el-Amarna
Limestone
Charles Amos Cummings Fund
1971.294

New Kingdom,
Dynasty XVIII,
reign of Akhenaten,
about 1363–1347 B.C.
H. 9⅜ in. (24 cm)

This relief presents a sensitive portrait of the eldest daughter of Akhenaten, standing behind her mother, Queen Nefertiti, whose figure is mostly lost. The princess wears a very large circular earring. Her crown and forehead are shaved, and she models a small wig that seems to have been altered anciently from a coiffure in another style. Although her neck and fingers are unusually thin, they present an image of grace and poise. The princess is shown in the act of presenting a large cone of scented fat to the Aten.

Fragmentary Head of a Prince or Princess

Limestone
Emily Esther Sears Fund, Maria Antoinette
Evans Fund, and Museum of Fine Arts
Egyptian Expedition Funds all by exchange
1976.602

New Kingdom,
Dynasty XVIII,
reign of Akhenaten,
about 1363–1347 B.C.
H. 6⅛ in. (15.5 cm)

This is an outstanding portrait in limestone of a member of the court of the late Amarna period at the end of Dynasty XVIII. Although the nose and the left side are missing, the face has a dreamlike, sensuous cast and conveys the ethereal, haunting beauty occasionally achieved by the master sculptors of the Amarna age. The pupils of the eye were once painted black, and the lips are painted red. Traces of red also remain in one of the nostrils.

One is tempted to speculate on the identity of the individual. Akhenaten is excluded; Nefertiti is a possible choice, although the cheeks are fuller and the chin more rounded than in most of her portraits. In view of the date at the very end of the Amarna age, we might even consider the princes who later ruled as Smenkhkare and Tutankhamen. It is still more likely that the head represents one of the six daughters of Akhenaten and Nefertiti, several of whom were destined to become queens in the waning years of the dynasty. In their childhood they are shown with elongated skulls, both in statuary and relief, but this feature did not survive into the final years at Amarna.

Relief of Tjawy

From Dra Abu el-Naga
Limestone
Edward J. and Mary S. Holmes Fund
1972.651

New Kingdom,
late Dynasty XVIII,
about 1402–1303 B.C.
H. 33½ in. (85 cm)

This Egyptian relief derives from the chapel of a royal cup bearer named Tjawy and represents him and members of his family and his servants. Two scenes are of exceptional interest. In the second register from the top, Tjawy superintends the measuring of grain for the serpent goddess Weret-Hekau. Her granary is shown on the right with four trees in the forecourt and six heaps of grain inside. In the center a statue of the goddess stands on a pedestal with a priest offering incense. The second scene depicts a seated harper at his instrument with a female harper, lute player, and clapping woman below. The artistry of the sculptor is particularly telling in the faces of the seated members of the family to the right of the musicians.

Lid for Ushabti Coffin

From Memphis
Limestone
William Francis Warden Fund
1977.717

New Kingdom
Dynasty XVIII,
reign of Horemheb,
about 1333–1303 B.C.
H. 12³/₁₆ in. (31 cm)

The lid of this double ushabti coffin bears representations of "the royal scribe and chief steward of Memphis," Iniuya, and his wife Iuy, "the songstress of Amen." The official served under the successors of Tutankhamen. His duties involved the supervision of the royal dockyards and arsenal at Memphis, from which military campaigns departed from Palestine and Syria. Iniuya's sarcophagus and the miniature brick pyramid that stood atop his Memphite tomb are in the Louvre. Decorated pillars from the same tomb are in Berlin, reliefs are in the Egyptian Museum in Cairo, and yet other elements are in Chicago. The subtly carved faces of husband and wife are practically duplicates, with the wife's face a trifle more feminine. Double and even triple ushabtis are known, but this double coffin and lid are unique in conception. The lid was brought from Egypt by General Jean-Joseph Tarayre (1770–1855), governor of Suez, and a friend of Napoleon. It remained with his family until purchased by the Museum of Fine Arts.

Mummy Shroud

Paint on gessoed linen
William Stevenson Smith Fund
1981.657

New Kingdom,
late Dynasty XVIII to early Dynasty XIX,
about 1310–1275 B.C.
H. 12¾ in. (32.4 cm)

Similar painted portraits have been found on the wooden coffins of officials buried at the workmen's village of Deir el-Medineh in Dynasties XVIII and XIX. It seems miraculous that this, and the several other examples exposed in such a fashion have survived the dust and insects for over three thousand years. The scene depicts the owner seated on a high-backed chair and extending his left hand to partake of the fruit and cakes on the table before him. The large almond-shaped eye, sloping nose, pert mouth, and the scented cone of fat on the carefully curled wig are all characteristic of late Dynasty XVIII. The colors are as vivid as they were on the day of interment. Evidently the painter enjoyed adding details to the fruit and cakes, tying the supporting strut to the chair, and enlivening each fingernail with a dab of white pigment. The necropolis workman who inscribed the hieroglyphs made several errors and even neglected to fill in the name of the deceased in the short text: "Anubis, lord of the necropolis, may he grant the inhalation of the sweet breeze (of the north)."

Relief of Mes

From Saqqara
Limestone
Helen and Alice Colburn Fund
1974.315

New Kingdom,
Dynasty XIX,
reign of Ramesses II
about 1250 B.C.
H. 14⅞ in. (38 cm)

The relief of Mes from his tomb at Saqqara is a notable example of early Ramesside carving. This well-known tomb was dismantled in the middle of the last century. A long text from it in the Cairo Museum, one of the most celebrated accounts of a legal dispute about agricultural land, has been studied by several generations of Egyptologists.

In the present relief, Mes is shown wearing flowing garments and is represented with the shaven head of a priest raising his hands in reverence to the goddess Isis; he is designated as the scribe of the treasury of Ptah. Between him and the goddess is an altar piled high with food and floral offerings. The features of the faces of the official and the goddess are in the fine post-Amarna style characteristic of the best Ramesside relief work. The pendant scene on the right is lost except for part of the figure of the goddess Nephthys.

Satirical Ostracon

Limestone
Mary Smith Fund
1976.784

New Kingdom,
Dynasty XIX–XX,
about 1303–1085 B.C.
H. 4⅞ in. (12.5 cm)

Egyptian artists saw humor in everyday life and were not averse to reproducing it in art. The humor in Egyptian art is perhaps nowhere better observed than in the freest of all artists' expressions, the so-called ostraca, a corpus of drawings made on smooth white limestone flakes. These flakes with their playful pictures, found tossed aside in the debris at the base of the Theban mountain, are like torn pages from the artists' sketchbooks. They had no public function, other than to amuse the artist's own circle. Some of the drawings are serious studies, or copies of formal compositions on tomb or temple walls. Others seem to satirize the formal art motifs. These often depict animals, dressed in human costume and poses, engaging in human pursuits. If the theme were not already droll enough, the scenes also present these animal characters in ludicrous role reversals, suggesting that these drawings may illustrate specific incidents in a cycle of animal fables and that the ostraca themselves may have served a need not unlike the modern comic book, whose animal characters are also entangled in a web of human predicaments.

In the present ostracon, an artist has drawn a cat in the role of a harried servant, carrying a wine cup and dish to an impatient mouse, seated lordlike on a fine stool, his feet resting on a footrest, and clad in a fine pleated linen garment, looking just like so many eminent nobles of the day as painted on the walls of their tombs. The fragmentary inscription overhead, referring to "the cat," may mimic a typical tomb text. Below this pair, a cat pads along to the left, bearing on his back the unlikely burden of a nest filled with newly hatched ducklings. This animal seems to be the very same creature so often depicted in marsh scenes as the one that robs the birds' nests of their young.

50

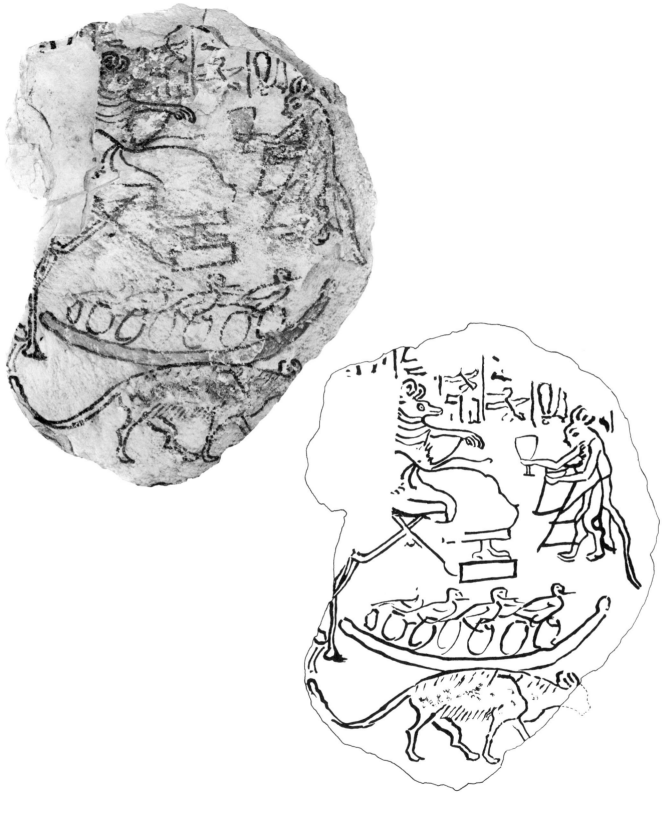

5 CM.

Sistrum

From Thebes
Bronze
Edward J. and Mary S. Holmes Fund
1970.572

New Kingdom,
Dynasty XXI–XXVI,
about 1085–525 B.C.
H. 17¼ in. (44 cm)

The handle of this exceptionally fine sistrum or ceremonial rattle is surmounted by addorsed Hathor heads. Its arc is fitted with three copper rods that pass through holes in the loop. They support tiny metal discs that tinkled when the sistrum was shaken. Cross-pieces and discs are restorations.

The image of the goddess has the usual ears of a cow, but the incised details of her curled wig and beaded collar are extraordinarily rich. On her shoulders are cobras with the crowns of Upper and Lower Egypt; a row of cobras with solar discs similarly adorns her platform crown; and six cobras superimposed in pairs disguise the sockets for the cross-pieces. Within the loop a single, rearing serpent coiffed in lappet wig, solar disc, and horns may represent a secondary image of Hathor.

On the sides of the loop the goddess Mut, Mistress of Ishru, is shown in the guise of a musician-priestess shaking two sistra before Amen-Re, Lord of the Thrones of the Two Lands, portrayed as a recumbent Libyan ram. The presence of the two deities suggests the sistrum came from one of the temples in the precinct of Amen at Karnak.

Statuette of a Kneeling King

Probably from Heracleopolis
Bronze
Edward J. and Mary S. Holmes Fund
1977.16

Third Intermediate Period,
about 750–725 B.C.
H. 8⅝ in. (22 cm)

This unusually fine bronze statuette represents a kneeling king. His costume consists of a close-fitting cap crown, encircled by a wide diadem with a single cobra, and a pleated *shendyet* kilt. Incised on each wrist is a bracelet, and around his neck is a choker necklace. Four rectangular tangs indicate that the figure was fixed in a separate base and probably formed part of a composite group that showed the royal postulant before his god. A cult object, now lost, may have been held between the extended hands.

A cartouche on the figure's belt identifies him as "Neferkare." The peculiar form of the crown he wears must assign the piece to the late Third Intermediate Period. These two clues make it fairly certain that he is Neferkare Pef-tjau-auwy-Bast, who ruled the city of Heracleopolis during the troubled times at the end of the late eighth century B.C. This king's name is also preserved on a magnificent gold statuette of the ram-headed god of Heracleopolis, Harsaphes, now in the museum, which was found by Petrie in the ruins of the city in 1904.

Our only historical glimpse of this little-known ruler is provided by the triumphal stele of Piye ("Piankhy"), king of Kush, who states that when he invaded Egypt (about 723 B.C.), Neferkare Pef-tjau-auwy-Bast came forth from his town, offering "gold, silver, all kinds of precious stones, and the best horses of his stable" to the conqueror, before whose feet "he threw himself on his belly." It is in this undignified pose that he was represented by Piye's artists both on the top of the stela, now in Cairo, and on the walls of the Great Amen Temple at Gebel Barkal in the Sudan.

56

Amulet of a Nubian Lady

Faience
William Stevenson Smith Fund
1984.168

Third Intermediate Period
Dynasty XXV,
about 760–656 B.C.
H. 5½ in. (14.2 cm)

Throughout the course of Egyptian art and literature the representation of foreigners is a favorite theme. This Nubian lady holding a basket with a child on her back is a well-known genre figure of that type. The un-Egyptian hairdo and the monkey and basket at her feet convey a certain element of humor in a caricature of a southerner.

The date suggested above is based on the occurrence of the similar hairdo of a sphinx or lion with a woman's head found at el-Kurru in the Sudan.

Block Statue of Djed-Ptah-ef-ankh

Probably from Thebes
Red quartzite
Gift of Mr. and Mrs. Donald Edgar
through Egyptian Curator's Fund
1971.21

Third Intermediate Period,
Dynasty XXV,
about 716–656 B.C.
H. 10½ in. (26.7 cm)

This fine statuette shows the official Djed-Ptah-ef-ankh seated on the ground with knees drawn up in front of him. The whole figure is enveloped in a cloak with only the hands projecting. The right hand holds a lettuce, which is associated with fertility and resurrection. Hanging from a cord around the neck is a pendant in the form of the *bat*-amulet, a curious emblem representing a human head in full face with cow ears and stylized horns and a knot or bow in front. Djed-Ptah-ef-ankh's thick, broad nose and heavy lips suggest association with the Kushite nobility from the south. The warm red quartzite is an attractive material for the portrait of the man and the inscriptions, which provide his name, offices, and parentage, and the information that the statue was dedicated by his son, Ankh-pa-khred.

Block statues were commonly placed as *ex-votos* in temples to enable an official to enjoy perpetual participation in the rituals and festivals. Djed-Ptah-ef-ankh's statue may have graced the temple of Amen-Re at Karnak.

Relief of a Divine Votaress and the Goddess Hathor

From Thebes
Sandstone
Egyptian Special Purchase Fund
1981.3

Dynasty XXV–XXVI,
about 760–525 B.C.
H. 19⅞ in. (51 cm)

In the late eight century B.C., Kushite kings from the far south conquered Egypt and united it with the Sudan as one kingdom. At this time the important positions of "God's Wife" and "Divine Votaress" in the Temple of Amen at Karnak were given to a daughter of the king, so that she might maintain control of the powerful Egyptian clergy. During the ensuing Dynasty XXVI, the practice was continued.

This relief depicts the goddess Isis (or Hathor) on the right, offering the symbol of life to a lady identifiable through her regalia as a divine votaress. The goddess wears a simple full wig with a uraeus or cobra at the forehead, surmounted by a modius or platform crown displaying a solar disk between a pair of horns. The votaress, on the other hand, wears the vulture headdress on which rises a Hathorian crown composed of solar disk, cow horns, and the feathers of a falcon. One lappet of her long wig hangs over her front shoulder. Both figures wear broad collars.

Although the lady has been identified as Amenirdis, daughter of the Kushite king Taharqa (about 690–664 B.C.), she may well represent a divine votaress of Dynasty XXVI, since the relief closely resembles a stela in the British Museum that represents the Divine Votaress Ankhnesneferibre, a daughter of Psamtik II (about 594–588 B.C.).

Stela of Iret-Hor-sekheru

From Thebes
Limestone
Egyptian Curator's Fund
1980.166

Dynasty XXV–XXVI,
about 670–660 B.C.
H. 15 in. (38.1 cm)

This funerary stela is made of very compact limestone. It has the customary rounded top beneath which is shown the sun's disk with outspread wings, representing the god Horus of Behdet, lord of the sky. Below this, and executed in a high relief, with rounded edges is a scene showing Iret-Hor-sekheru, the man commemorated, with his arms raised in praise before the enthroned god Osiris. On the right his father, Djed-Khonsu-ef-ankh, similarly praises the enthroned falcon-headed god Re. Both father and son wear cones of scented fat on their heads. An offering table with breads and a lotus flower is placed in front of each of the gods. The accompanying text expresses the wish that Iret-Hor-sekheru traverse the heavens, travel among the imperishable stars, and never die.

Male Head

Dark schist
Egyptian Curator's Fund
1984.406

Late Period
early Dynasty XXVI,
seventh century B.C.
H. 3¾ in. (9.5 cm)

In the dynasties following the New Kingdom, and especially during the Kushite and Saite dynasties, Egyptian sculpture develops along traditional lines and also shows tendencies reflecting foreign influence. The head presented here is notable for its veristic details, including an emphasis on signs of age and exaggeration of the features. The thin-lipped mouth with downward lines at the corners, the sinus pouches over the cheek bones, shown as heavy drooping folds, and the exaggerated slanting ridges rising on the temples from the root of the nose indicate the preoccupation on the part of the sculptor with flesh and skin. The conventional bag wig and ears set off a dour, uncompromising expression emphasized by the damage done to the nose. On the back support there are traces of two columns of hieroglyphic text, of which the first is the beginning of the standard offering formula and the second is entirely effaced.

Statue of a Vizier

Dark green schist
William E. Nickerson Fund
1970.495

Late Period,
Dynasty XXVI,
reign of Psamtik I,
about 664–609 B.C.
H. 19^{11}/$_{16}$ in. (50 cm)

The vizier is shown with his hands at his side and his left foot advanced in the classic attitude of a striding man. He wears the formal *shendyet*-kilt with central tab and plain belt. His ears are entirely covered by a valanced wig without curls. The modeling of the body is very fine with almost mannerist features: extremely long arms, a full and fleshy chest with sculptured nipples, collar bones extending over the shoulders, a muscular torso with strong bipartition, a narrow waist, and a youthful, idealizing face. The base of the statue is missing as is the name of the owner at the bottom of the series of titles on the back support. Nonetheless, the titles correspond so closely to the series of titles and name in the great tomb of Bakenrenef at Saqqara that it seems likely the statue represents the well-known vizier of Psamtik I. The lower legs, feet, and base are restored.

Plaque

From Mit Rahineh (Memphis)
Bronze
Egyptian Curator's Fund
1982.180

Late Period,
Dynasty XXVI,
about 664–525 B.C.
H. 8 in. (20.3 cm)

This openwork bronze plaque represents the corpulent Nile god Hapy, holding a tray of jars, hung with papyrus and lotus flowers. Beneath the tray is the silhouette of a cartouche, although due to the slightly encrusted condition of the object, the royal name is not visible.

The plaque undoubtedly derives from the hoard of forty-two bronzes discovered by Daninos Pacha at Mit Rahineh (ancient Memphis) during the winter of 1900–01. These were all elements of sacred furniture and temple utensils that had evidently been hastily buried for concealment. Several related to the cult of Amen, and it would thus appear that they were of Theban origin. Some were acquired by the Cairo Museum, but other plaques from this series have long been in the collections of the Walters Art Gallery, Baltimore, and several other museums.

From the knob preserved above Hapy's head, it is clear that the Boston plaque ornamented a box. A cord wound around it and another knob in a corresponding position on the lid would have secured the box. Many of the objects in the Mit Rahineh hoard preserve royal names and those of the "Divine Votaresses of Amen," indicating that they were produced during Dynasties XXV and XXVI. The latest royal name is that of Amasis (about 568–526 B.C.), and it seems likely that these objects were buried to protect them from the invading armies of Persia in 525 B.C.

Cosmetic Box with Crouching Frog on lid

Said to be from Mersin near Adana
in Southwest Turkey
Green faience with details in blue
Edward J. and Mary S. Holmes Fund
1970.571

Dynasty XXVI,
about 664–525 B.C. or
earlier
H. 1⅞ in. (5.4 cm)

Said to have been found in Anatolia, the green faience box may have been a wedding gift for a noble lady. Egypt exported luxury wares to the Mediterranean world at this time. The frog on the lid guards the contents with his legs alert and ready to spring. The bulging belly contrasts with the head and its fierce expression. The lid is secured by a peg and the box arranged in four interior compartments.

Footcase of a Mummy

Cartonnage
Arthur Mason Knapp Fund
1971.217

Roman Period,
first century A.D.
H. 7½ in. (19 cm)

In Egyptian iconography the victorious king is repeatedly shown trampling on his enemies. Images of bound captives were often placed on the soles of his sandals. In later times, the same iconography was extended to the dead and may be seen, for example, on the cartonnage footcases of the mummies bearing the well-known face panels of the type known as "Fayum portraits."

On the bottom of the sandals in this fine footcase appear two bound and tied captives; on the left, a brown Nubian and on the right, a red Asiatic. It seems obvious here that the traditional enemies of Egypt have been reinterpreted as representatives of the evil powers of the underworld. Trampled underfoot, they are obviously helpless.

On the upper surface of the footcase two sandal-clad feet, modeled in high relief, are painted bright pink with gilded toenails. Green rosettes with red centers around the border further enliven its appearance.

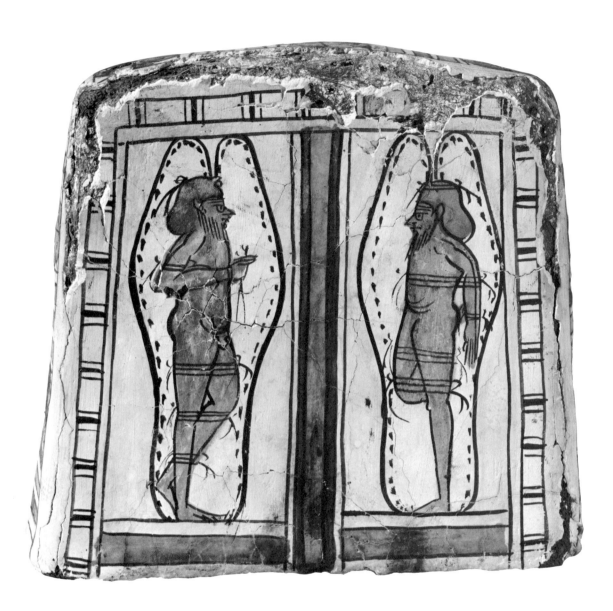

Inlay

Mosaic glass
Gift of John Jermain Slocum
1972.229

First century B.C. to first
century A.D.
H. ⅝ in. (1.5 cm)

In its colors and details, this prize plaque is a masterwork of the glassmaker's trade. The sacred eye of Horus in the center, a potent amulet used to ward off evil, is flanked by three identical figures of the god Heh, personification of infinity, kneeling on the hieroglyph for gold and clasping notched palm-ribs, the ancient Egyptian symbol for a multitude of years.

It is very likely that the plaque ultimately derives from a small shrine or *naos*, which housed the cult statue of some god. Generally such shrines were made of wood, so they could be placed on sacred boats at the great festivals, when processions were formed and the priests took the shrine on their shoulders to be shown to the multitudes. The wooden surface of the *naos* was covered with gold leaf and encrusted with faience and glass inlays, often worked into elaborate figural compositions but also with decorative and amuletic borders. It was from one of those borders that this inlay doubtless came.

Tomb Statue of a Woman

From Behnesa (Oxyrhynchos)
Limestone, with traces of paint
Edward J. and Mary S. Holmes Fund
1972.875

Roman Period,
late second to third century A.D.
H. 55½ in. (141 cm)

The lady portrayed here was probably an Egyptian Greek and a citizen of the town of Oxyrhynchos in Middle Egypt, which came into prominence in the Graeco-Roman period. Oxyrhynchos was a cult center of Isis, and both her costume of long tunic and knotted cloak, as well as the heavy garland she wears over one shoulder identify her as a devotee of the mother goddess. In her left hand the lady carries a bowl of sacred Nile water, while her right hand held a situla or libation vessel now broken off. Her jewelry, a heavy necklace and pendant earrings painted yellow in imitation of gold, indicates that she was probably a member of a wealthy family of the town. The statue almost certainly stood in a niche from which it was broken in ancient or modern times. The head is damaged but seems never to have been intended as a true portrait.

Mummy Mask

Gilded plaster
Edward J. and Mary S. Holmes Fund
1977.175

Roman Period,
early third century A.D.
H. 7½ in. (19 cm)

Mold-made plaster mummy masks became increasingly popular as burial equipment while Egypt was under Roman rule, and illustrate the degree to which traditional Egyptian customs were altered in this cosmopolitan age. Even the provincial arts were influenced by the Imperial court as illustrated in this mask, which sports a beard and hairstyle made popular by the Emperor Hadrian.

The beard and facial features were cast and then covered with a thin layer of brown clay, which served as a ground for the gold leaf applied to the surface. The eyes are composed of calcite and the irises are clear glass with a painted backing. The pupils are of obsidian set in gold casings. The corners of the eyes were painted red with a lead pigment and held in a copper setting with the edges serrated to imitate lashes.

Although the features on these mass-produced masks are clearly influenced by Roman sculpture, they continue the idealizing traditions of Egyptian funerary art.

Funerary Stela of Heraklides

Probably from Kom Abou Billou,
Western Delta
Limestone
Marilyn M. Simpson Fund
1984.256

Roman Period,
third to fourth century A.D.
H. 13⅛ in. (33.3 cm)

The stela depicts a man lying on a couch dressed in an Ionic chiton and himation. In his hand he holds a two-handled libation cup in typical Greek pose. To his right is a representation of the Egyptian jackal-god Anubis on a standard. The whole composition is framed within two lotus columns and an elaborate pediment. Beneath the couch are represented two sheaves of wheat and an offering table. The inscription in two lines of lightly incised Greek at the base of the stela begins: "Heraklides, devoted to his brothers and devoted to his children . . ."

Such stelae were usually placed within a niche in the facade of the mud brick superstructure of a Roman Period tomb. They appear to have been mass produced; the name, age, and sometimes the profession of the deceased were added at the time of burial.

Fragment of a Stone Beaker

From South Central Iran
Chlorite
Egyptian Special Purchase Fund
1980.71

Early Dynastic II,
about 2800–2600 B.C.
H. 7 in. (18 cm)

This fragmentary stone beaker is carved in relief in the so-called "International Style" of Western Asia. Fragments of similar vessels have been found throughout Mesopotamia, in the islands of the Persian Gulf, on the Iranian steppe, and even in the Indus Valley, all in contexts dating to the period 2800–2600 B.C. The stone itself, a greenish black chlorite, is widely distributed throughout the Zagros mountains, and one ancient mine has even been identified in the vicinity of Tepe Yahya in south central Iran, where such vessels were clearly carved and shipped east and west. These objects were doubtless luxury items sought by the Sumerian elite, for in Mesopotamia they have only been found in rich burials, temples, and palaces.

The relief depicts a fantastic being with human head and torso, with a bull's head for a waist and claws as feet, grasping two snakes by the neck. On the opposite side a human figure with knee-length skirt, standing atop a hut, holds two lions upside down. The lions, in turn, grasp the snakes held by the other figure, creating a continuous frieze of grappling figures reminiscent of designs on Early Dynastic II cylinder seals. The vessel preserves about half of an inscription in archaic Sumerian, cut over the figure standing on the hut. This states that the object was "dedicated (to) the 'high house of Engur' (for) Engur, (god of) the totality of the Sea-Land." If "Engur" is an alternate reading for the name of "Enki," the water god, as it is thought to be, this object may thus have been dedicated to the chief deity of the city of Eridu in southern Mesopotamia, which in the early third millennium B.C. was a thriving seaport near the mouth of the Euphrates and the Persian Gulf.

Bust of a Babylonian Priestess or Votaress

From Mesopotamia   Isin-Larsa Period,
Terracotta   about 2000–1800 B.C.
Edward J. and Mary S. Holmes Fund   H. 15 in. (38 cm)
1972.870

In 1972 the museum acquired a trio of early Mesopotamian terracottas: a statuette of a seated dog wearing a wide collar and two slightly less than life-size female heads, one emerging from a round base, and this object, which takes the form of a bust set on an oval base. All three were made of a coarse, chaff-tempered marl clay and fired. The two heads are hollow, having been formed around a removable central, probably wooden, support. Thermoluminescence dating indicated that all were contemporary and were made in the early second millennium B.C.

The subject of the bust is a broad-shouldered, thick-necked, buxom lady, wearing a high neckband. Her breasts are artificially high and accentuated by what appears to be the collar of a dress conforming exactly to the curvature of the body. Her shoulder-length hair is held in place by a fillet encircling the crown of the head and by a hairnet, which is indicated by crisscrossing diagonal lines. Traces of paint indicate that the fleshy face was colored a reddish-brown and the hair, black.

Pieces closely related to this are in the Ashmolean Museum, the Baghdad Museum, the British Museum, the Royal Ontario Museum, and the Norbert Schimmel Collection in New York. That these sculptures were made only as heads or busts on flat bases rather than as complete figures suggests that they were intended to be set on benches or pedestals or within niches. Most likely they represent priestesses or female votaries and were dedicatory sculptures set up in a temple of the Isin-Larsa Period. The associated dog statuettes suggest that the deity worshipped in the shrine was the healing goddess Gula, whose sweet nature and devotion to mankind was symbolized by the faithful canine.

Cuneiform Tablet with Seal of Ini-Teshub, King of Carchemish

From North Syria
Clay
Frank Bemis Fund
1977.114

Hittite,
about 1250 B.C.
H. 3½ in. (8.75 cm)

Ini-Teshub was the Hittite viceroy in North Syria during the mid-thirteenth century B.C. This tablet is a record of a lawsuit heard before him, in which is recorded the testimony of two quarreling merchants in a case involving an unpaid debt. It is written in Akkadian (Babylonian), the international language of the Late Bronze Age. In its center is a fine, bold impression of the king's magnificent stamp seal, inscribed with his name and title in both cuneiform and the Hittite hieroglyphic script, and bearing the figure of a Hittite god holding a winged sphinx in an outstretched arm.

88

Pair of Blinkers from a Horse Harness

From Eastern Anatolia
Bronze
Egyptian Curator's Fund and gift of Mrs.
Horace L. Mayer and William Kelly Simpson
1977.489
William Stevenson Smith Fund
1981.83

Urartian,
seventh century B.C.
H. 3½ in. (9 cm)
H. 3¾ in. (9.5 cm)

Made to protect the eyes of a chariot horse, this extraordinary pair of blinkers bears a mirror image design in relief that perfectly illustrates the Urartian predilection for artistic themes of animals and combat. In a tense blend of action and repose, a lion-centaur, helmeted, bearded, and winged, springs toward a beardless sphinx. Framed by ringlets and perched between outstretched wings, the sphinx's head protrudes from the surface of the metal in such high relief as to give the impression of being virtually in the round. One would suspect that it had been cast and applied separately, yet examination of the reverse reveals that it, too, was done in repoussé—no mean feat when the thickness of the metal is considered. This unusual feature, the uniformly good modeling of the figures, and the delicate chasing of their surface details are all indicators of Urartian toreutic work in its highest form.

90

Vessel with Bull's-Head Protomes

From Eastern Anatolia
Ceramic
Morris and Louise Rosenthal Fund
and Egyptian Curator's Fund
1981.654

Urartian,
late ninth to seventh century B.C.
H. 13¾ in. (35 cm)

Once considered a common class of Urartian pottery, the dazzling "red-polished ware" is now known to have been a luxury ceramic used almost exclusively in the great royal residences. Rarely found in the ruins of the provincial fortresses or town sites, it has been excavated in greatest quantities from the magazines of the major Urartian palaces at such sites as Van Kalesi and Toprakkale near Lake Van in eastern Turkey, at Karmir-Blur near Erevan, Soviet Armenia, and at Bastam in northwestern Iran. The vessels assume a variety of shapes, normally with unusual sculptural features, and all would seem to be inspired by metal prototypes. The modeled projecting bulls' heads imitate the more realistic protomes frequently found adorning the rims of Urartian bronze cauldrons. The fluting on the sides is also typical of metal vessels dating from the later Achaemenian period and thereafter.

Earring

From Iran
Gold cloisonné with inlays of
turquoise, lapis lazuli, and carnelian
Edward J. and Mary S. Holmes Fund
1971.256

Achaemenid Period,
about 525–330 B.C.
Diam. 1¹⁵⁄₁₆ in. (5 cm)

This sumptuous earring, the mate to one in the Norbert Schimmel Collection in New York, is a gold disk, partitioned with a dense web of cloisonné inlays of turquoise, lapis lazuli, and carnelian. The front and back are treated with equal care and each side once bore the extraordinary number of 229 inlays. Today only about half remain. Each surface displays a central roundel ornamented with the torso of a bearded regal figure emerging from a crescent with a tail and two pairs of wings. Around this figure are seven smaller roundels: six contain male figures emerging from crescents, each facing the central figure, and the seventh bears a lotus blossom and crescent. Recent research has shown that the design closely parallels that carved in relief over the tombs of Darius the Great and his successors at Persepolis and would seem to symbolize the Zoroastrian concept of the order both of the earth and the universe. It probably represents at once the king himself being revered by the six Great Houses of the empire, the land of Persia surrounded by the six great world regions, and the god Ahuramazda surrounded by the six lesser divinities known as the Bounteous Immortals. The lotus blossom of the seventh roundel may imitate the similar Egyptian symbol, which identified the king as sun over all, or it may have symbolized the watery eighth world region, the Ocean.

Amulet Depicting the Demon Lamashtu

Northwestern Iran
Polished black stone, with reddish
white paste filling incised lines
Horace and Florence Mayer Fund
1985.103

Neo-Assyrian,
ninth to seventh century B.C.
H. 1½ in. (3.8 cm)

Like the peoples of many traditional cultures even today, the Assyrians and their neighbors believed that medical problems were the result of supernatural evil forces, against which the sufferers were helpless to defend unless they enlisted the aid of professional exorcists and used appropriate amulets and other ritualistic paraphernalia. In antiquity one of the most potentially dangerous periods for women was the time of pregnancy and birth, and to ensure against complications it was necessary to protect oneself against the hag demon Lamashtu, who was thought to enter the home silently during birth and to kill newborn infants in order to take them unto herself. This amulet, representing the lion-headed, bird-clawed Lamashtu, would have been worn by an expectant mother to defend herself against this creature, who was always depicted as a hideous caricature of motherhood, suckling a dog and a pig from her pendant breasts. Here she even appears to be pregnant herself. As we know from a cuneiform tablet in the Louvre, which preserves the ritual against Lamashtu, she was bribed away from the expectant mother with offerings of such small feminine objects as combs and fibulae. These objects and a clay image of the demon were set adrift on river or canal in a model boat, on which she was supposed to make her way back to the land of the dead whence she came. The amulet depicts an appeased Lamashtu sailing away in her boat, holding in her hands her new comb and fibula.

Pitcher with Frieze of a Goddess Hunting Animals

From Central Anatolia
Buff ware, painted brown and red
Edward J. and Mary S. Holmes Fund
1971.297

Late Phrygian,
about 625 B.C.
H. 11¾ in. (30 cm)

This vessel, with its painted frieze of the Anatolian mother goddess Kubaba (Cybele), is probably the most important Late Phrygian vessel that has yet been found. Its importance even in antiquity is indicated by the fact that in ancient times, after having been broken, it was painstakingly repaired with lead clamps, suggesting that it had an indispensable ritual use and very likely formed part of a temple service. The goddess, drawing a bow, showers the leopard before her with arrows, while a goat stands behind her, and a griffon, with a bird's head on the end of its tail, stands in front of the leopard. Although the provenience of the vessel is unknown, it was very likely a place having trade relations with northern Syria, since the bird-headed tail of the griffin is a motif often encountered in north Syrian art. The motif of a goddess having mastery over leopards and lions is a most ancient one in Anatolian art, first appearing in the art of the aceramic Neolithic of the mid-seventh millennium B.C.

98

Helmet

Probably from Iran
or Eastern Turkey
Brass
Morris and Louise Rosenthal Fund
1979.41

Parthian,
first century B.C. to
fourth century A.D.
H. 13¼ in. (34 cm)

This helmet, with its elaborate chased patterning apparently imitating a quilted fabric, was clearly inspired by the peculiar oriental headdress known as the *kidaris*, which had been very much in vogue at least as early as the seventh century B.C. among nomadic Eastern peoples from the Danube to Mongolia. Although metal helmets of comparable type are known from Thrace and the Black Sea littoral as early as the fifth century B.C., this particular helmet is most similar to those headdresses represented in the art of the Parthian period, such as those adorning the sculptures on the monumental tomb of Antiochus I of Commagene (69–34 B.C.) at Nemrut Dagh, those worn by the priests in the "fresco of Conon" (about A.D. 70) at Dura Europus, or those represented in certain royal statuary of second century date from Hatra.

Perhaps the most remarkable parallel to this helmet, though, is that found on a sculpture of one of the west Indian Scythian rulers of Kushan (about first to fourth centuries), now in the Mathura Museum in India. Although lacking the rosettes on the sides and peak, the headdress worn by this figure bears identical patterning on the surface. Made entirely of brass, the Museum's helmet is the only known surviving example of its type.

Bowl with Ram on a Mountaintop

From Iran
Silver with details mercury gilded
J.H. and E.A. Payne Fund
1971.52

Sasanian Period,
fifth to seventh century A.D.
Diam. 8¼ in. (21.2 cm)

The subject of this silver plate is a mountain sheep stepping nimbly across flower-covered peaks to sniff a magical blossom. This is no ordinary animal but a symbol of royalty. Around his neck is a studded bell collar trailing the same fluttering ribbons so often depicted streaming from the king's crown and the royal vestments shown on similar vessels. The ram, in fact, was a symbol of the fortune of Ardashir, founder of the Sasanian Dynasty, symbolism which was perpetuated in the *Shahnama*. The amuletic value of the ram's image was doubtless the reason for its frequent use as a design on Sasanian seals. At least two of the Sasanian monarchs incorporated ram's horns into their crowns.

The body, head, horns, and blossom have been separately fashioned and applied to the surface as raised relief. The animal and the blossom have been mercury gilded.

References

Page 2   Whitney M. Davis, "An Early Dynastic Lion in the Museum of Fine Arts," *Studies in Ancient Egypt, the Aegean, and the Sudan: Essays in honor of Dows Dunham on the occasion of his 90th birthday, June 1, 1980*, ed. William K. Simpson and Whitney M. Davis (Boston: Museum of Fine Arts, Department of Egyptian and Ancient Near Eastern Art, 1981), pp. 34–42; Museum of Fine Arts, Boston, *Annual Report*, 1979–80, p. 22.

Page 4   Museum of Fine Arts, Boston, *Annual Report*, 1972–73, pp. 49–50; Bertha Porter and Rosalind Moss, *Topographical Bibliography of Ancient Egyptian Hieroglyphic Texts, Reliefs, and Paintings*, vol. 1 (Oxford: Clarendon Press, 1960), pp. 391–393; Elizabeth Riefstahl, "Two Hairdressers of the Eleventh Dynasty," *Journal of Near Eastern Studies* 15 (1956): 10–17; William K. Simpson, *The Face of Egypt: Permanence and Change in Egyptian Art*, Katonah-Dallas exhibition catalogue, 1977, no. 13, pp. 25, 67; William K. Simpson, "The Middle Kingdom in Egypt: Some Recent Acquisitions," *Boston Museum Bulletin* 72, no. 368 (1974): 105–108.

Page 6   William K. Simpson, "The Middle Kingdom in Egypt: Some Recent Acquisitions," *Boston Museum Bulletin* 72, no. 368 (1974): 104–105; idem, "Recent Museum Acquisitions: Egyptian and Ancient Near Eastern Art in Boston, 1970–71," *Burlington Magazine* 114 (April 1972): 237–242; Edward Terrace, "An Age of Reflection: The Egyptian Middle Kingdom in Boston," *Connoisseur* (August 1968), pp. 265–272.

Page 8   Museum of Fine Arts, Boston, *Annual Report*, 1982–83, p. 24.

Page 10   William K. Simpson, "The Middle Kingdom in Egypt: Some Recent Acquisitions," *Boston Museum Bulletin* 72, no. 368 (1974): 109–111.

Page 12   William Hayes, "Egyptian Sculpture: A Statue of the Lady Senewy," *Art in America* 35 (October 1947): 256–263.

Page 14   William K. Simpson, "The Lintels of Si-Hathor-Nehy in Boston and Cairo," *Revue d'Egyptologie* 24 (1972): 169–175; idem, "The Middle Kingdom in Egypt: Some Recent Acquisitions," *Boston Museum Bulletin* 72, no. 368 (1974): 108–109.

Page 16   Museum of Fine Arts, Boston, *Annual Report*, 1972–73, pp. 49, 51; William K. Simpson, "The Middle Kingdom in Egypt: Some Recent Acquisitions," *Boston Museum Bulletin* 72, no. 368 (1974): 100–104; Dietrich Wildung, *Sesostris und Amenemhet*, Munich: Hirmer, 1984, p. 162.

Page 18   William K. Simpson, "Acquisitions in Egyptian and Ancient Near Eastern Art in the Boston Museum of Fine Arts, 1970–71," *Connoisseur* 179 (February 1972), 3:116–117.

Page 20   Georges Daressy, *Cercueils des cachettes royales*, Catalogue des antiquités égyptiennes du Musée du Caire, vol. 50 (Cairo: Institut français d'archéologie orientale, 1909), pl. 2, pp. 1–2; Museum of Fine Arts, Boston, *Annual Report*, 1980–81, p. 20.

Page 22   Museum of Fine Arts, Boston, *Annual Report*, 1982–83, p. 25.

Page 24   William K. Simpson, "Egyptian Statuary of Courtiers in Dynasty 18," Museum of Fine Arts, Boston, *Bulletin* 77 (1979): 37–40.

Page 26   Museum of Fine Arts, Boston, *Annual Report*, 1977–78, p. 26; Museum of Fine Arts, Boston, *Egypt's Golden Age: The Art of Living in the New Kingdom 1558–1085 B.C.*, exhibition catalogue, 1982, p. 142.

Page 28   William K. Simpson, "Egyptian Statuary of Courtiers in Dynasty 18," Museum of Fine Arts, Boston, *Bulletin* 77 (1979): 37–40; idem, "The Middle Kingdom in Egypt: Some Recent Accessions," *Boston Museum Bulletin* 70, no. 359 (1972): 116–117.

Page 30   Museum of Fine Arts, Boston, *Annual Report*, 1980–81, p. 20; William K. Simpson, "A Stela of the Chief Coppersmith Ahmose," *Mélanges Offerts à Jean Vercoutter* (Paris: Editions Recherche sur les civilizations, 1985), pp. 312–316.

Page 32   William K. Simpson, "Egyptian Statuary of Courtiers in Dynasty 18," Museum of Fine Arts, Boston, *Bulletin* 77 (1979): 45–46.

Page 34   Museum of Fine Arts, Boston, *Annual Report*, 1984–85, p. 28; Museum of Fine Arts, Boston, *Egypt's Golden Age: The Art of Living in the New Kingdom 1558–1085 B.C.*, exhibition catalogue, 1982, pp. 293–294.

Page 36   William K. Simpson, "Egyptian Statuary of Courtiers in Dynasty 18," Museum of Fine Arts, Boston, *Bulletin* 77 (1979): 46–47; idem, *The Face of Egypt: Permanence and Change in Egyptian Art*, Katonah-Dallas exhibition catalogue, 1977, no. 25, p. 34.

Page 38 Cyril Aldred, *Akhenaten and Nefertiti*, catalogue of an exhibition celebrating the 150th anniversary of the Brooklyn Institute of Art and Sciences (New York: The Brooklyn Museum in Association with the Viking Press, 1973), no. 124, p. 193; Gunther Roeder, *Amarna - Reliefs aus Hermopolis* (Hildesheim: Gerstenberg, 1969); John D. Cooney, *Amarna Reliefs from Hermopolis in American Collections* (Brooklyn, N.Y.: The Brooklyn Museum, 1965), no. 17, pp. 29–30; William K. Simpson, "Century Two: Collecting Egyptian and Ancient Near Eastern Art for the Boston Museum," *Apollo* 98 (1973): 250–257.

Page 40 Museum of Fine Arts, Boston, *Annual Report*, 1976–77, p. 29; William K. Simpson, "Egyptian Statuary of Courtiers of Dynasty 18," Museum of Fine Arts, Boston, *Bulletin* 77 (1979): 48–49; idem, *The Face of Egypt: Permanence and Change in Egyptian Art*, Katonah-Dallas exhibition catalogue, 1977, no. 21.

Page 42 J.J. Clère, "La table d'offrandes de l'échanson royal Sa-Rénénoutet surnommé Tchaouy," *Bulletin du Centenaire* (Suppl. BIFAO 1981), pp. 213–234; Museum of Fine Arts, Boston, *Annual Report*, 1971–72, pp. 51, 54; William K. Simpson, "A Relief of the Royal Cup-Bearer Tja-wy," *Boston Museum Bulletin* 71, no. 360 (1973), pp. 69–82.

Page 44 Museum of Fine Arts, Boston, *Annual Report*, 1977–78, p. 26; William K. Simpson, "A Shawabti Box Lid of the Chief Steward Nia (Iniuya) Acquired by General Jean-Joseph Tarayre," *Bulletin du Centenaire* (Suppl. BIFAO 1981), pp. 325–329.

Page 46 Bernard Bruyère, *Rapport sur les fouilles de Deir el-Médineh* vol. 6, pt. 2, (Cairo: Institut français d'archéologie orientale, 1929), pl. 111; William C. Hayes, *The Scepter of Egypt*, vol. 2, (New York: Metropolitan Museum of Art, 1959), fig. 202, p. 320; Museum of Fine Arts, Boston, *Annual Report*, 1981–82, p. 27.

Page 48 G.A. Gaballa, *The Memphite Tomb-Chapel of Mose* (Warminster: Aris and Phillips, 1977), pl. XXX, p. 15; Alan H. Gardiner, *The Inscription of Mes* (Leipzig: J.C. Hinrichs, 1905); Museum of Fine Arts, Boston, *Annual Report*, 1973–74, p. 9; Bertha Porter and Rosalind Moss, *Topographical Bibliography of Ancient Egyptian Hieroglyphic Texts, Reliefs, and Paintings, Memphis*, vol. 3, (Oxford: Clarendon Press, 1931), pp. 553–555.

Page 50 Museum of Fine Arts, Boston, *Annual Report*, 1976–77, p. 41; David P. Silverman, in *Egypt's Golden Age: The Art of Living in the New Kingdom 1558–1085 b.c.*, exhibition catalogue, 1982, no. 383, pp. 279–280.

Page 52 William K. Simpson, "Century Two: Collecting Egyptian and Ancient Near Eastern Art for the Boston Museum," *Apollo* 98 (1973): 25.

Page 54   Museum of Fine Arts, Boston, *Annual Report*, 1976–77, p. 28; Edna Russman with Lambertus van Zelst, "An Egyptian Royal Statuette of the Eighth Century B.C.," *Studies in Ancient Egypt, the Aegean, and the Sudan: Essays in honor of Dows Dunham on the occasion of his 90th birthday, June 1, 1980*, ed. William K. Simpson and Whitney M. Davis (Boston: Museum of Fine Arts, 1981), pp. 149–156.

Page 58   Dows Dunham, *El Kurru* (Cambridge: Harvard University Press, 1950), pl. 55, p. 78; Museum of Fine Arts, Boston, *Annual Report*, 1983–84, p. 25.

Page 60   William K. Simpson, "Acquisitions in Egyptian and Ancient Near Eastern Art in the Boston Museum of Fine Arts, 1970–71," *Connoisseur* (February 1972): 118; idem, "Three Egyptian Statues of the Seventh and Sixth Centuries B.C. in the Boston Museum of Fine Arts," *Kêmi* 21 (1974): 17–25.

Page 62   Museum of Fine Arts, Boston, *Annual Report*, 1980–81, p. 21; William K. Simpson, "A Relief of a Divine Votaress in Boston," *Chronique d'Egypte* 57 (1982): 231–235.

Page 64   Peter Munro, *Die spätägyptischen Totenstelen*, (Gluckstadt: Verlag J.J. Augustin, 1973), p. 206; Museum of Fine Arts, Boston, *Annual Report*, 1979–80, p. 23.

Page 66   Museum of Fine Arts, Boston, *Annual Report*, 1984–85, p. 29.

Page 68   Bernard Bothmer, "The Brussels-Brooklyn Statue of Bakenrenef," in *Mélanges Gamal Eddin Mokhtar*, vol. 1, (Cairo: IFAO, 1985), p. 100; J.J. Clère, "Une Statuette du Vizir Bakenrénef," in *Studia in Honorem Bernardi V. Bothmer* (Brussels: Musées Royaux d'Art et d'Histoire, 1983), pp. 25–26; William K. Simpson, "Recent Museum Acquisitions: Egyptian and Ancient Near Eastern Art in Boston, 1970–71," *Burlington Magazine* 114 (April 1972): 237–242; idem, "Three Egyptian Statues of the Seventh and Sixth Centuries B.C. in the Boston Museum of Fine Arts," *Kêmi* 21 (1971): 25–30.

Page 70   Georges Daressy, "Une Trouvailles de Bronzes à Mit Rahineh," *Annales du Service des Antiquitiés de l'Egypte* 3 (1902): 139–150; *The New Brummer Collection*, Ancient Art, vol. 11, (Zurich: Koller, Spink, and Son, 1979), pp. 56–57.

Page 72   Museum of Fine Arts, Boston, *Annual Report*, 1970–71, p. 46; Museum of Fine Arts, Boston, *The Rathbone Years*, exhibition catalogue, Boston 1972, p. 26; William K. Simpson, "Acquisitions in Egyptian and Ancient Near Eastern Art in the Boston Museum of Fine Arts, 1970–71," *Connoisseur* 179 (February 1972): 118–119.

Page 74 William K. Simpson, "Acquisitions in Egyptian and Ancient Near Eastern Art in the Boston Museum of Fine Arts, 1970–71," *Connoisseur* 179 (February 1972), nos. 9, 9a; idem, "Ptolemaic-Roman Cartonnage Footcases with Prisoners Bound and Tied," *Zeitschrift für Ägyptische Sprache und Altertumskunde* 100 (1973): 50–54.

Page 76 John Cooney, "An Egyptian Mosaic Glass Panel," *Boston Museum Bulletin* 74, no. 370 (1976): 111–114.

Page 78 William Culican, "Acquisitions from Egypt and Syria," *Art Bulletin of Victoria* 1973–74: 20–26; Museum of Fine Arts, Boston, *Romans and Barbarians*, exhibition catalogue, Department of Classical Art, Boston, 1976, no. 32; Hans Schneider, *Beelden van Behnasa*, (Zutphen: Terra, 1982), pp. 39–50; J. Vandier, "Nouvelles Acquisitions, Musée du Louvre," *La Revue du Louvre et des Musées de France* (1972): 190–192.

Page 80 Museum of Fine Arts, Boston, *Annual Report*, 1976–77, p. 41.

Page 82 Zaki Aly, "Some Funerary Stelae from Kon Abou Bellow," *Bulletin of the Société Royale d'Archéologie—Alexandrie, Bulletin* 38 (1949): 55–88; Zahi Hawwass, "Preliminary Report on the Excavations at Kom Abou Bellow," *Studien zur Altägyptischen Kultur* 7 (1979), pp. 75–88; Finley Hooper, *Funerary Stelae from Kom Abou Bellow*, Ann Arbor: University of Michigan, 1961.

Page 84 P. Amiet, "Antiquités du désert de Lut. II," *Révue d'assyriologie et d'archéologie orientale* 70 (1976): 1–8; Holly Pittman, *Art of the Bronze Age: Southeastern Iran, Western Central Asia, and the Indus Valley* (New York: The Metropolitan Museum of Art, 1984), p. 70.

Page 86 Museum of Fine Arts, Boston, *Annual Report*, 1972–73, pp. 48–49.

Page 88 Museum of Fine Arts, Boston, *Annual Report*, 1976–77, p. 29; David Owen, "A Legal Text from the Court of Ini-Teshub," *Oriens Antiquus* 28 (in press).

Page 90 Museum of Fine Arts, Boston, *Annual Report*, 1976–77, p. 28; Museum of Fine Arts, Boston, *Annual Report*, 1980–81, p. 36.

Page 92 Museum of Fine Arts, Boston, *Annual Report*, 1981–82, p. 26.

Page 94 J.F.X. McKeon, "Achaemenian Cloisonné-Inlay, an Important New Example," *Orient and Occident: Essays Presented to Cyrus H. Gordon on the Occasion of his*

Sixty-Fifth Birthday, ed. H.A. Hoffner (Neukirchen-Vluyn: Verlag Butzon & Bercker, 1973), pp. 109–117; Oscar Muscarella, ed., *Ancient Art: The Norbert Schimmel Collection*, (Mainz: P. von Zabern, 1974), p. 156; A.S. Shahbazi, "'Darius' Haft Kishvar," *Kunst, Kultur, und Geschichte der Achämenidzeit und ihr Fortleben* (Archäologische Mitteilungen aus Iran: Erganzungsband 10), (Berlin: Reimer Verlag, 1983), pp. 239–246; W.J. Young, "The Fabulous Gold of the Pactolus Valley," *Boston Museum Bulletin* 70, no. 359 (1972): 5–8.

Page 96 Museum of Fine Arts, Boston, *Annual Report*, 1984–85, p. 28.

Page 98 Lilly Kahil, "Artémis," *Lexicon Iconographicum Mythologiae Classicae*, vol. II, pt. 1, (Zurich and Munchen: Artemis Verlag, 1984), p. 633; Timothy Kendall, "A Late Phrygian Pitcher," *Boston Museum Bulletin* 73, no. 369 (1975): 30–33; Museum of Fine Arts, Boston, *The Rathbone Years*, exhibition catalog, Boston, 1972, p. 32; William K. Simpson, "Century Two: Collecting Egyptian and Ancient Near Eastern Art in the Boston Museum," *Apollo* 98 (1973): 256.

Page 100 Museum of Fine Arts, Boston, *Annual Report*, 1978–79, p. 23.

Page 102 Museum of Fine Arts, Boston, *Annual Report*, 1970–71, p. 46; Museum of Fine Arts, Boston, *Romans and Barbarians*, exhibition catalogue, Department of Classical Art, Boston, 1976, no. 219; Parke-Bernet Galleries, Inc., *Egyptian, Western Asiatic, Greek, and Roman Antiquities*, sales catalogue, 1966, no. 147; William K. Simpson, "Acquisitions in Egyptian and Ancient Near Eastern Art in the Boston Museum of Fine Arts, 1970–71," *Connoisseur* 179 (February 1972): 120.